INVENTOR?

REFERENCE BOOKS

WORKSHOP SPACE

SECRET PLANS

IGNORED

SCIENTIST

CURIOUS

WHO WAS THE REAL HEDY LAMARR?

To my daughters, Kim and Lisa.
—L.W.

For my friend, Rosie.
—K.W.

union square kids

NEW YORK

UNION SQUARE KIDS and the distinctive Union Square Kids logo are trademarks of Union Square & Co., LLC.

Union Square & Co., LLC, is a subsidiary of Sterling Publishing Co., Inc.

Text © 2019 Laurie Wallmark
Cover and interior illustrations © 2019 Katy Wu

ISBN 978-1-4549-2691-7

For information about custom editions, special sales, and premium purchases, please contact specialsales@unionsquareandco.com.

Printed in China

Lot #:
6 8 10 9 7

03/23

unionsquareandco.com

The art for this book was created digitally.
Design by Irene Vandervoort

HEDY LAMARR'S

DOUBLE LIFE

WRITTEN BY

LAURIE WALLMARK

ILLUSTRATED BY

KATY WU

union
square
kids

NEW YORK

Hedy Lamarr led a double life. The public knew her as a glamorous movie star, famous throughout the world. But in private Hedy was a brilliant inventor, a fact known only to her closest friends.

Hedy's greatest invention was the technology known as frequency-hopping spread spectrum. This is the scientific breakthrough that helps keep our cell phone messages private and defends our computers from hackers. Without Hedy's revolutionary idea, the electronic devices we use every day would be more open to attack.

Cameras flashed. The glamorous movie star stepped out of her limousine and onto the red carpet. Everyone who was anyone in Hollywood was there. The star-studded premiere of her first English-language movie, *Algiers*, was the social event of 1938.

Journalists and photographers crowded around her. If they only knew the story, the true story, behind the world's most beautiful woman.

"PEOPLE SEEM TO THINK BECAUSE I HAVE A PRETTY FACE I'M STUPID.... I HAVE TO WORK TWICE AS HARD AS ANYONE ELSE TO CONVINCE PEOPLE I HAVE SOMETHING RESEMBLING A BRAIN."

The Hollywood legend had no interest in a glitzy lifestyle. Her passion was science and engineering. Hedy converted her fancy parlor into an inventor's workshop, complete with tools, a drafting table, and many well-thumbed technical books. After long days of acting, Hedy hurried home to work on her latest invention.

Her brain overflowed with idea after idea for useful inventions.

Though Hedy never tried to sell any of these inventions, that didn't stop her from working to make her designs the best they could be.

THIRSTY TRAVELERS?
Hedy made a flavor-cube that changed plain water into soda.

"INVENTIONS ARE EASY FOR ME TO DO. I SUPPOSE I JUST CAME FROM A DIFFERENT PLACE."

A DEVICE TO HELP PEOPLE IN AND OUT OF THE BATHTUB

LOST PETS?
She designed a glow-in-the-dark dog collar.

AN ACCORDION-FOLD POCKET ON TISSUE BOXES
Hedy intended them to hold used tissues.

A NEW TRAFFIC SIGNAL
It would indicate when the light was about to change.

Even as a child in Austria in the early 1920s, Hedy's curious mind wanted to know how things worked. What powered automobiles? Which type of motor worked best in an airplane? How could she improve a machine's design? At age five, Hedy took apart her music box to examine the mechanism.

Hedy's father shared her love of science and technology. During their walks around their hometown of Vienna, Austria, they exchanged ideas about everything and anything. From streetcars to printing presses, and even the constellations that dotted the night sky, Hedy wanted to understand the science and technology behind them all.

Young Hedy was also crazy about motion pictures. Whenever possible, she sneaked off to a movie theater. Returning home, Hedy reenacted her favorite scenes, playing all the parts herself.

She constructed a stage for her dolls underneath her father's desk. There, she performed shows for imaginary audiences.

Her dolls starred as fairytale heroes and villains. For real audiences, Hedy acted in school plays and sang at music festivals.

Always dreaming, Hedy wanted to escape into the movies.

Soon she got her chance.

"ALL MY LIFE I HAD LOVED
TO PLAY ACT AND PRETEND."

Hedy's first job was as a script girl at a movie studio in Vienna. When the opportunity came up to be an extra in a movie, Hedy rushed to apply. She won a minor role in a restaurant scene. This bit part, small as it was, gave Hedy her first steps on the road to stardom.

Hedy constantly practiced her acting skills. She imitated family, friends, and even people she saw on the street. She mimicked the way people walked and talked. She copied their mannerisms and facial expressions.

"I ACTED ALL THE TIME.... I WAS A LITTLE
LIVING COPYBOOK. I WROTE PEOPLE DOWN ON ME."

Before long, Hedy was cast as the lead in a play. She caught the eye of a very famous Hollywood producer, Louis B. Mayer. Impressed by her talent, he offered her a seven-year movie contract. Hedy left her family behind in Europe and settled in America.

"MY FACE HAS BEEN MY MISFORTUNE... A MASK I CANNOT REMOVE. I MUST LIVE WITH IT. I CURSE IT."

STRANGE LOVES HIDING IN THE CASBAH CITY OF SECRETS!

CHARLES BOYER · HEDY LAMARR
ALGIERS

After only six months of English lessons, she starred in her first American movie.

Mayer thought a glamorous star needed a Hollywood name, so "Hedwig Eva Maria Kiesler" became "Hedy Lamarr."

Hedy went on to star in many well-loved films, including the biblical drama *Samson and Delilah* and the comedy *My Favorite Spy*. She acted with some of the most famous movie stars of the time, people like Angela Lansbury, Jimmy Stewart, Judy Garland, and Clark Gable. Hedy was now a major movie star.

"THE BRAINS OF PEOPLE ARE MORE INTERESTING THAN THE LOOKS, I THINK."

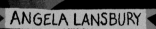
ANGELA LANSBURY

JIMMY STEWART

JUDY GARLAND

CLARK GABLE

Hedy's movies let people escape the talk of war, if only for a few hours. World War II was raging, and everyone was afraid. Nazis had taken over Germany, and Nazi soldiers had invaded many other European countries.

At a friend's dinner party, Hedy met George Antheil, a composer of modern music. She learned he was also a former weapons inspector. This reminded Hedy of a discussion she had overheard back in Europe about a problem with the guidance system for torpedoes.

"HOPE AND CURIOSITY ABOUT THE FUTURE SEEMED BETTER THAN GUARANTEES. THAT'S THE WAY I WAS."

The guidance system couldn't prevent the enemy from jamming the weapon's radio signals. Because of this, the enemy could command a torpedo to go off course. That would be disastrous.

Hedy asked George if the United States Navy faced a similar problem with their torpedoes.

They did.

The two inventors decided to combine their talents and figure out a solution to the problem. During breaks from inventing, they challenged each other with games on the piano.

George's hands hopped quickly from piano key to piano key. Hedy's hands flew across the keyboard, matching him note for note in a different octave.

With every different key she pressed, a piano wire quickly moved back and forth. The speed of the wire's movement, or its frequency, produced the correct note for that key.

Hedy realized that even though the notes were constantly changing, she and George could still play the same tune. All she had to do was match the notes' frequencies.

This gave her an idea.

The idea to build a *secure* torpedo guidance system.

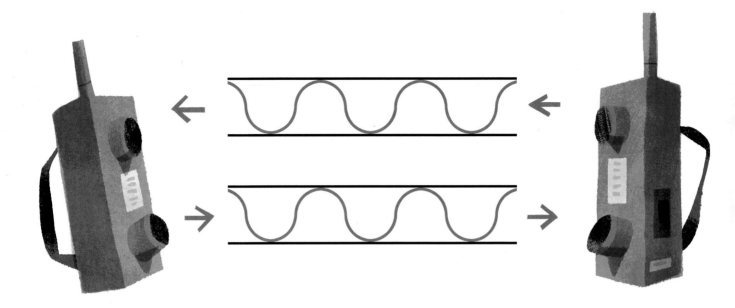

In the early 1940s, these guidance systems worked like a walkie-talkie, a two-way radio. In order for walkie-talkies to communicate, both handsets must be tuned to the same frequency. Like strings in a piano, radio waves between pairs of walkie-talkies have unique frequencies. A pair of walkie-talkies can only communicate when they are set to the same frequency.

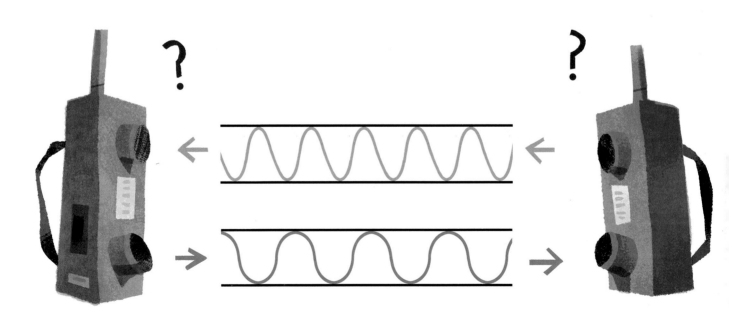

Torpedo guidance systems used to work like that: the equipment on a ship launching a torpedo and the torpedo itself needed to be set to the same frequency. If the enemy figured out what that frequency was, they could cause trouble.

Hedy proposed an improved system, one that worked as if it contained several pairs of walkie-talkies. Each pair would be set to a unique frequency. From moment to moment, the system could switch which pair of "walkie-talkies" carried the message.

" THE IDEA JUST CAME TO ME...
I NEVER THOUGHT OF SUCH A THING BEFORE
AND PROBABLY NEVER SHALL AGAIN."

F: Frequency

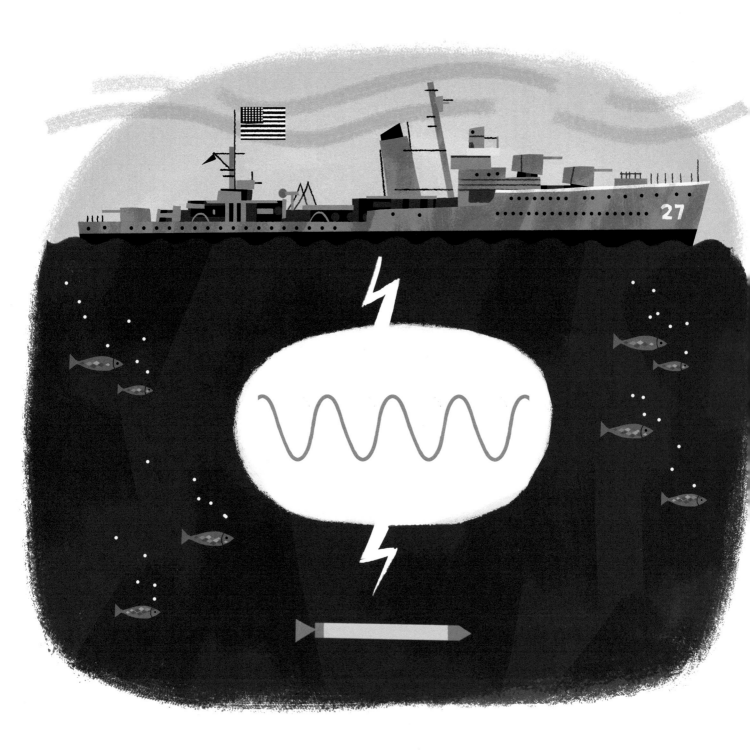

Hedy's system didn't actually contain numerous walkie-talkies.
Instead, it used a single device that could quickly change frequencies.
As long as the device on the ship and the one on the torpedo
were tuned to the same frequency at the same time, they could
communicate. Hedy called her discovery "the hopping of frequencies."

Hedy and George spent night after night brainstorming ways to implement her idea.

Frequency hopping was the most important part of the guidance system they developed. Even if the enemy managed to overhear part of a message, it didn't matter. The device had already hopped to a new frequency. Unless the enemy knew the frequency being used at an exact moment, they couldn't interfere with the message.

"I EXPLAINED THE BASICS OF THE IDEA, AND THE IMPLEMENTATION PART CAME FROM GEORGE."

Hedy and George added another security feature to their system. It broke messages into pieces and sent them in short bursts. These were so short the enemy might not even realize a message had been sent.

Hedy and George shared their idea with the National Inventors Council, the group that evaluated discoveries for possible military use. The council told them their idea had "great potential value" and was

"ALL CREATIVE PEOPLE WANT TO DO THE UNEXPECTED."

Their system still needed to be automated so it could work without a human at the controls. There had to be some way of making sure that both devices used the same frequency at the same time. Without this, the system would be useless.

Hedy remembered George had once arranged for sixteen player pianos to play at the same time. Moving rolls of paper with holes punched in them told the pianos which notes to play and when.

In Hedy and George's invention, matching rolls of ribbon on the ship and the torpedo controlled the system. The holes signaled which frequency the system should use at that time. That allowed the transmitter and receiver to change frequencies simultaneously.

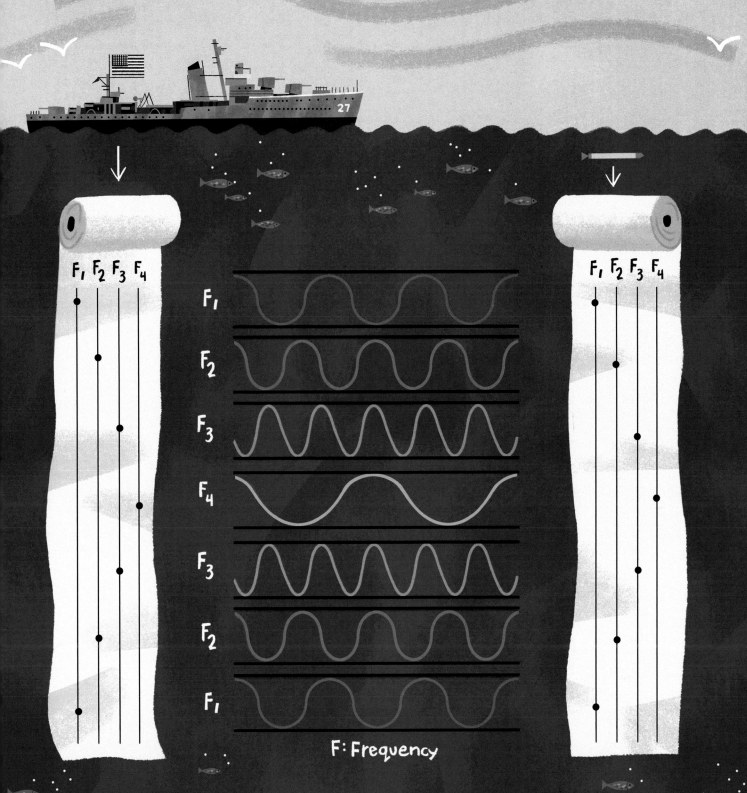

F: Frequency

"IMPROVING THINGS COMES NATURALLY TO ME."

After months and months of hard work, Hedy and George finished their secret communications system. They wrote a detailed description of the design and filled out an application for a patent. If the patent was approved, no one could steal Hedy and George's idea.

They sent their patent application to the government. Then they waited.

And waited.

And waited.

"DO GOOD ANYWAY...
THINK BIG ANYWAY...
BUILD ANYWAY..."

More than a year later, on August 11, 1942, they received their patent.

Frequency hopping, their technology-changing invention, was ready to share with the world.

They immediately handed both the idea and the patent to the United States Navy. Hedy was proud her frequency-hopping idea might help America win the war.

"WE WERE NOW AT WAR AND A TERRIBLE TIME IT WAS."

UNITED STATES PATENT OFFICE
SECRET COMMUNICATION SYSTEM
HEDY LAMARR,
GEORGE ANTHEIL

SECRET

Unfortunately, the Navy had neither the time nor the money to implement a new system during wartime. They refused to develop Hedy and George's invention. Even worse, they classified the technology SECRET. This prevented anyone, including the inventors, from using it.

Hedy looked for another way to help her adopted country defeat the hated Nazis. She realized she could use her celebrity to raise money by selling war bonds. Hedy traveled cross-country and held sales rallies. She sold 25 million dollars worth of war bonds.

Hedy also volunteered at the Hollywood Canteen, a club for American servicemen soon to be sent into battle. To lift their spirits, she chatted and danced with them. By the end of each evening, her feet were sore, but she was happy to have helped the soldiers and sailors.

No matter the job that needed to be done, the famous movie star was first in line to lend a hand. She even washed dishes. Friday nights at the Canteen became Hedy Lamarr Night.

When Hedy wasn't busy volunteering or acting, she continued to tinker in her inventor's workshop. More than twenty movies later, Hedy retired from acting.

Forty years later, the military finally declassified Hedy's frequency-hopping technology. The patent had long since expired, so anyone was now free to use this invention. They didn't need to give Hedy or George the credit for their amazing discovery.

Companies raced to include frequency hopping in their own devices. This technology can be found inside many of today's most popular electronics.

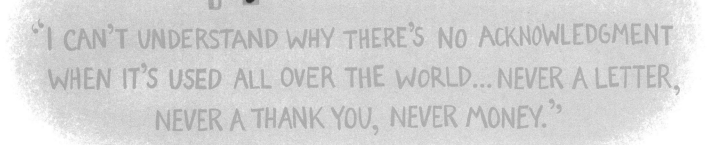

"I CAN'T UNDERSTAND WHY THERE'S NO ACKNOWLEDGMENT WHEN IT'S USED ALL OVER THE WORLD... NEVER A LETTER, NEVER A THANK YOU, NEVER MONEY."

Frequency-hopping spread spectrum is the technology that helps keep cell phone calls and texts private. It's the trick that allows secure wireless communications between computers and the Internet. And it makes it harder for people to hack drone aircraft.

All this was made possible by Hedy's idea, "the hopping of frequencies."

"MY LIFE WAS FULL OF COLORS, FULL OF LIFE....
I DON'T REGRET ANYTHING.... I LEARNED A LOT."

It wasn't until more than fifty years after their patent was granted that the world recognized the contributions of Hedy Lamarr and George Antheil. In 1997, the inventors received the Pioneer Award from the Electronic Frontier Foundation for their significant contribution to computers.

Hedy's response to this great honor?

"It's about time."

TIMELINE

November 9, 1914	Hedwig Eva Maria Kiesler is born in Vienna, Austria
October 4, 1937	Arrives in Hollywood and starts using her new name, Hedy Lamarr
March 12, 1938	*Nazis invade Austria ("Anschluss")*
August 5, 1938	Stars in her first English-language movie, *Algiers*
November 9–10, 1938	*Nazis attack Jews throughout Europe ("Kristallnacht")*
Summer, 1940	Meets George Antheil and discusses her interest in inventing
Fall, 1940	Works with George on invention to guide torpedoes
December 1940	Shares frequency-hopping design with the National Inventors Council
June 10, 1941	Applies for a patent for frequency hopping
December 7, 1941	*Japan bombs the Pearl Harbor Navy base in Hawaii*
December 8, 1941	*United States enters World War II*
January–February 1942	Navy classifies the torpedo guidance system as secret.
August 11, 1942	Receives patent #US2292387A
September 2, 1945	*World War II ends*
April 10, 1953	Becomes a United States citizen
1959	Patent expires
February 8, 1960	Inducted into Hollywood's Walk of Fame
October 16–28, 1962	*US torpedoes are equipped with frequency-hopping technology during the Cuban Missile Crisis, but no torpedoes are ever fired*
1981–1985	*Frequency hopping declassified for commercial use and military use*
1991	*First digital cell phone introduced*
March 20, 1997	Receives Electronic Frontier Foundation's Pioneer Award
January 19, 2000	Hedy Lamarr dies in Casselberry, Florida
2014	Inducted into the National Inventors Hall of Fame
April 2017	The documentary, *Bombshell: The Hedy Lamarr Story*, premieres

SECRETS OF THE SECRET COMMUNICATIONS SYSTEM

HEDY'S DISCOVERY, frequency-hopping spread spectrum, reduced the chances that a radio signal controlling a torpedo could be intercepted by someone else. It worked by constantly switching frequencies of wireless transmissions. Without knowing the correct frequency, the enemy wouldn't be able to block, read, or change a message.

But you can't get a patent just for having an original idea, no matter how good it is. You also have to show how your idea can work in the real world. And that's just what Hedy and George did. The two inventors engineered a practical design for their secret communications system.

Rolls of ribbons punched with holes controlled the system. Each row of holes corresponded to a different frequency. The ship's transmitter and the torpedo's receiver used identical ribbons to ensure they were set to the same frequency at the same time.

The system created hundreds of frequency hops per second. Even if the enemy correctly guessed the frequency being used, it didn't matter. The transmitter and receiver had already switched to another one. There was little chance the enemy could intercept the message.

The signals were sent in quick bursts. Each short message contained only one simple command to guide the torpedo, like turn left or dive deeper.

To confuse the enemy even more, some of the radio signals contained no information at all.

For the frequency hopping system to work, the transmitter and receiver had to change frequencies at the exact same moment. Matching holes on the two ribbons had to roll over control heads simultaneously.

To do this, Hedy and George added a start hole to the ribbons. Until it was time to launch the torpedo, a pin in these holes kept the ribbons motionless. As soon as the torpedo fired, the pins released, and the ribbons rolled.

Hedy and George's design for implementing frequency hopping was almost complete. There was still one problem, though. When they first developed their design, they imagined the ribbon to be like a player piano roll, with the ability to control 88 different frequencies. But a torpedo isn't large enough to handle this many.

They solved this problem by having seven frequencies for the transmitter, but only four for the receiver. The three extra frequencies sent dummy signals, which contained no real data. In fact, the Navy could even use these signals to send false information. If the enemy intercepted one of these fake messages, they wouldn't realize they were looking at garbage data.

Hedy and George's invention was finished. They had created a jam-proof torpedo guidance system.

More important, they invented a technology essential to many of the electronics we use every day.

SELECTED BIBLIOGRAPHY

Barton, Ruth. *Hedy Lamarr: The Most Beautiful Woman in Film.*
Lexington: University of Kentucky, 2010.

Rhodes, Richard. *Hedy's Folly: The Life and Breakthrough Inventions of Hedy Lamarr,
the Most Beautiful Woman in the World.*
New York: Doubleday, 2011.

Shearer, Stephen Michael. *Beautiful: The Life of Hedy Lamarr.*
New York: Thomas Dunne /St. Martin's, 2010.

Swaby, Rachel. *Headstrong: 52 Women Who Changed Science . . . and the World.*
New York: Broadway Books, 2015.

ADDITIONAL READING ABOUT OTHER WOMEN IN STEM

Burleigh, Robert, and Raúl Colón. *Solving the Puzzle under the Sea: Marie Tharp Maps the Ocean Floor.*
New York: Simon & Schuster Books for Young Readers, 2016.

Ignotofsky, Rachel. *Women in Science: 50 Fearless Pioneers Who Changed the World.*
New York: Wren & Rook, 2017.

Keating, Jess, and Marta Alvarez Miguens. *Shark Lady: The True Story of How Eugenie Clark
Became the Ocean's Most Fearless Scientist.* Naperville, IL: Sourcebooks Jabberwocky, 2017.

McCully, Emily Arnold. *Caroline's Comets: A True Story.*
New York: Holiday House, 2017.

Robbins, Dean, and Lucy Knisley. *Margaret and the Moon: How Margaret Hamilton
Saved the First Lunar Landing.* New York: Alfred A. Knopf, 2017.

Shetterly, Margot Lee, et al. *Hidden Figures: the True Story of Four Black Women and the Space Race.*
New York: Harper, an Imprint of HarperCollins Publishers, 2018.

Wallmark, Laurie and April Chu. *Ada Byron Lovelace and the Thinking Machine.*
Berkeley, CA: Creston Books, 2016.

Wallmark, Laurie and Katy Wu. *Grace Hopper: Queen of Computer Code.*
New York: Sterling Children's Books, 2017.